49 Sender: Réquiem por un campesino español

GW00648550

Critical Guides to Spanish Texts

EDITED BY J.E. VAREY, A.D. DEYERMOND & C. DAVIES

SENDER

Réquiem por un Campesino Español

Stephen M. Hart

Associate Professor of Spanish
University of Kentucky

Grant & Cutler Ltd 1996

© Grant & Cutler Ltd 1996

ISBN 0 07293 0304 7

First edition 1990
Reprinted with corrections and a revised bibliography 1996

DEPÓSITO LEGAL: V. 27 - 1996

Printed in Spain by
Artes Gráficas Soler, S.A., Valencia
for
GRANT AND CUTLER LTD
55-57 GREAT MARLBOROUGH STREET, LONDON, W1V 2AY

Contents

For Dany

Prefatory Note

Sender's novel *Mosén Millán* was first published in Mexico by Aquelarre in 1953. It was subsequently re-published in New York by Las Américas in 1960 in a bilingual edition with the new title *Réquiem por un campesino español* and with a prologue by Mair José Benardete. The latter is now regarded as the correct title, although some studies still refer to the former title of the novel (see Bibliographical Note). As a condition before he returned to Spain, Sender required that all of his works be granted permission to be published there. The first Spanish edition was that of Barcelona: Destino, 1974. Numerous reprintings of this work have followed. All subsequent reprints of the novel by Destinolibro have been dedicated to Jesús Vived Mairal, a post-Conciliar Spanish priest Sender met in Spain in 1974 (*21*, pp. 84-86). The edition used throughout this study is *Réquiem por un campesino español*, 10th edition (Barcelona: Destino, 1984). References to this work are given in parentheses after each quotation. Figures in parentheses in italic type refer to the Bibliographical Note; where necessary they are followed by page numbers. I take this opportunity to express my profound gratitude to Professor J.E. Varey and Professor A.D. Deyermond for their instructive comments made on a first draft of this study.

1. Plot, Realism and Anti-Realism

The Plot

The plot, described as a 'simple and moving tale' by Emir Rodríguez Monegal (5, p. 23), can be summarized quite quickly. The novel describes the thoughts which pass through the mind of a priest, Mosén Millán, as he prepares to conduct a Requiem Mass for one of his parishioners, Paco el del Molino, who was executed by the Nationalist army a year before, at the outbreak of the Civil War during the summer of 1936. The priest's thoughts are interrupted by three main events; firstly, the periodic entrance of the altar-boy into the sacristy where the priest is sitting, in order to inform him that nobody has yet arrived; secondly, the arrival of the three rich men of the village, don Valeriano, don Gumersindo and Cástulo Pérez, each of whom offers to pay for the Mass (Mosén Millán refuses the offer in each case); and thirdly, the mysterious entrance of Paco's colt into the church, and the eventually successful efforts made by the three rich men and Mosén Millán to get rid of the colt. These, then, are the three main events which occur within the present, and which interrupt the priest's recollections. Mosén Millán's thoughts constitute a reconstruction of Paco's life centring on the four main events in which the priest was personally involved, namely, Paco's baptism, his confirmation at the age of seven, his marriage to Agueda, and his execution by the Nationalist army at the outbreak of the Civil War.

The novel clearly works on two temporal levels, which are the past (the salient features of Paco's life), and the present (those minutes before the Mass begins when Mosén Millán is sitting in the sacristy). An important link between these two temporal levels is provided by the ballad dedicated to Paco el del Molino, and which

the altar-boy, and occasionally Mosén Millán himself, hum. The
ballad serves a variety of functions. Firstly, it is by means of this
ballad, as Patricia McDermott points out, that 'Paco passes into folk
history as a hero and a martyr, into the eternity of myth'; it equally
fulfills a function of interior duplication 'pointing to the process
that is going on in the novel itself: the preservation of memory
through the creation of poetic history and myth' (*35*, p. 56).
Secondly, as Robert G. Havard has suggested, the *romance* has 'the
precise function of jogging Mosén Millán's memory, with the
monaguillo's awareness of this being not entirely innocent. A
definitive pattern emerges: the priest recalls a sequence of Paco's
life; he returns to the present to ask if any villagers have arrived to
attend the Mass; the *monaguillo* replies in the negative and then
recites a piece of the *romance* which prompts further recall on the
part of Mosén Millán' (*30*, p. 91). The two levels of past and
present are harmonized neatly at the end of the novel. The *romance*
ends, the account of Paco's death follows, and the Requiem Mass
begins. A close parallel is suggested between the ballad and the
Mass in that, as Havard argues, the *romance* is the 'villagers' own
secular requiem for Paco' (*30*, p. 90).

Often the transition between past and present is presented as a
smooth flow of association between ideas. A good example of this
device occurs early in the text (p. 13). Mosén Millán notices that
his shoes need repairing; he thinks of sending them to the
shoemaker (who is new in the village), which leads him to think of
the previous shoemaker (a good friend of Paco's), and his
recollections begin. Another example of smooth transition may be
found on page 66:

> Hubo un largo silencio. Don Valeriano arrollaba su
> cadena en el dedo índice y luego la dejaba resbalar. Los
> dijes sonaban. Uno tenía un rizo de pelo de su difunta
> esposa. Otro, una reliquia del santo P. Claret heredada
> de su bisabuelo. Hablaba en voz baja de los precios de
> la lana y del cuero, sin que nadie le contestara.

> Mosén Millán, con los ojos cerrados, recordaba aún el día de la boda de Paco. En el comedor, una señora había perdido un pendiente, y dos hombres andaban a cuatro manos buscándolo. Mosén Millán pensaba que en las bodas siempre hay una mujer a quien se le cae un pendiente, y lo busca, y no lo encuentra.

In an almost Proustian way, the jangling of don Valeriano's medallions hanging round his neck reminds Mosén Millán of a lost ear-ring at Paco's wedding. The silence mentioned at the beginning of the passage is the pause which causes Mosén Millán's thoughts to wander. While it is clear that Mosén Millán is an incorrigible daydreamer (fifty-one years' officiating had created 'un automatismo que le permitía poner el pensamiento en otra parte sin dejar de rezar', p. 10), his memories serve an important function in this novel, not only in reconstructing the past but in throwing light on his psychology. Firstly, they show how the priest uses memory as a means of protecting himself against the demands of the present: 'Se entretenía Mosén Millán con aquellas memorias para evitar oír lo que decían don Gumersindo y don Valeriano' (p. 67). Secondly, the very persistence of these memories suggests, paradoxically enough, that Mosén Millán is trying desperately to come to terms with his feelings, and resolve the guilt caused by the role he played in Paco's execution. *church is guilty.*

Realism

Realism is the favoured mode for description of the priest's memories. The flashbacks are normally preceded by the preliminary verb 'recordaba'. In the first use of this technique in the novel, the scene turns into a third-person narrative of seemingly objective validity, immediately after the magic word 'recordaba' appears:

> Recordaba Mosén Millán el día que bautizó a Paco en
> aquella misma iglesia. La mañana del bautizo se
> presentó fría y dorada, una de esas mañanitas en que la
> grava del río que había puesto en la plaza durante el
> Corpus, crujía de frío bajo los pies. Iba el niño en
> brazos de la madrina, envuelto en ricas mantillas, y
> cubierto por un manto de raso blanco, bordado en sedas
> blancas, también. (p. 13)

If one adopts René Wellek's working definition of realism as 'the
objective representation of contemporary social reality',[1] it is clear
that the style in which Mosén Millán's memories are presented is
indeed realistic. The description of the weather and the child's
baptismal garments is seemingly based on objective observation.
An element of social reality is evident in the description of the
custom in this particular village of spreading gravel extracted from
the river bed on the town square during the festival of Corpus
Christi.

   Such a depiction of local customs is a distinctive feature of
Sender's realism as articulated in *Réquiem*. This has led one critic
to speak of *costumbrismo* in this novel, *costumbrismo* being
understood as a type of realism which is specifically concerned
with the depiction of customs in rural regions of Spain (see *13*, p.
77, and *36*, pp. 110-11). However, there is one important difference
between Sender's description of village customs and traditional
costumbrismo. In the nineteenth century, *costumbrismo* was
politically associated with the rural way of life and it consequently
expressed a conservative and reactionary ideology.[2] Sender's use of
such rural customs is quite different, for they are presented as a

---

[1] 'The Concept of Realism in Literary Scholarship', in his *Concepts of
Criticism* (New Haven: Yale University Press, 1963), pp. 222-55 (pp. 240-
41). For further discussion of Sender's use of 'recordar' and its relation to
realism, see *22*, p. 130.

[2] D.L. Shaw, *A Literary History of Spain: The Nineteenth Century*
(London: Ernest Benn, 1972), p. 45.

secular and popular culture set up against the traditional values of the Church (see pp. 35-39, below). The reference to popular customs in the text fulfills a dual purpose. Firstly, it satisfies one of the prerequisites of realism, namely, that the text should give the optical illusion of being based on an objective social reality. Secondly, it harmonizes successfully with the repetitive mode of the text. For just as Mosén Millán's memories re-enact Paco's life, and commemorate the past, so these events commemorate the repetitive aspects of human behaviour within a community.

Sender's own type of realism can be differentiated from what he has called bourgeois realism, as is evident from his article 'El novelista y las masas' published in *Leviatán* in 1936:

⚹ Lo que diferencia el realismo burgués del nuestro es que nosotros vemos la realidad dialécticamente y no idealmente. Nuestro realismo no es sólo analítico y crítico como el de los naturalistas, sino que parte de una concepción dinámica y no estática de la realidad. Nuestra realidad, con la que no estamos satisfechos sino en cuanto forma parte dinámica de un proceso en cambio y avance constante, no es estática ni produce en nosotros la ilusión de la contemplación neutra. (quoted in *12*, p. 181)

Sender's dialectical realism is thus at the furthest remove from *costumbrista* writing in its depiction of a dynamic, constantly changing reality (see *37* for further discussion of this point). Sender's text is, likewise, often full of gaps which problematize its status as a medium which refers to an empiric reality. This is echoed by the frequent references throughout the novel to confusion, disorientation and the breakdown of communication. Language is apt to conceal rather than reveal, especially in the tense political atmosphere of the Republic when, as Peter A. Bly points out, 'the respective leaders of the growing social and political antagonisms display the highest degree of mutual incomprehensibility' (*23*, p. 97). The breakdown in communication between individuals in the novel itself constitutes an image in miniature of the problematic status of realism. The gap between reality and the language which purports to describe that reality was an issue close to Sender's heart. He hinted at this when he defined realism as follows: 'Es simplemente la manera de usar de la realidad como un pequeño instrumento que nos permite dar el salto en el vacío y despertar o sugerir en el lector cosas que no había percibido antes' (*17*, p. 234). Sender's dialectical realism is thus centred on an awareness of the gap between language and reality.

Anti-Realism

Sender's desire to force the reader to perceive more than the visible subverts, at times, the conventions of realism and, in particular, the unspoken rules underlying first-/third-person narrative. Often, for example, Mosén Millán's act of memory can lead to a chain of events in which the priest himself is depicted as existing independently of the subjective act of memory. The reader is thereby jolted because she is carried along by the flow of Mosén Millán's memories, only to find that the overall author has taken overt control of the narrative as an omniscient narrator. Consider the following passage, which is typical of many of its kind throughout the narrative:

> Recordaba Mosén Millán que sobre una mesa había un paquete de velas rizadas y adornadas, y que en un extremo de la habitación estaba la cuna del niño. A su lado, la madre, de breve cabeza y pecho opulento, con esa serenidad majestuosa de las recién paridas. El padre atendía a los amigos. Uno de ellos se acercaba a la cuna, y preguntaba: - ¿Es tu hijo? - Hombre, no lo sé - dijo el padre acusando con una tranquila sorna lo obvio de la pregunta -. Al menos, de mi mujer sí que lo es. Luego soltó la carcajada. Mosén Millán, que estaba leyendo su grimorio, alzó la cabeza: - Vamos, no seas bruto. ¿Qué sacas con esas bromas? (p. 15)

Mosén Millán's words, which express his dislike of sexual innuendo during a baptismal celebration, jolt the narrative in that they are presented objectively, even though they form part of his subjective memory. For, because of the opening words of the passage 'Recordaba Mosén Millán que...', the reader will have assumed that the events subsequently described are the priest's memories. This is clearly shown not to be the case when the priest suddenly speaks. And, yet, it is nowhere explicitly stated that we have passed from the plane of the priest's memory to an omniscient third-person narrative. This narrative technique, called 'objective restrospection' by Darío Villanueva, is, in fact, the hallmark of the style of *Réquiem* (*7*, p. 264). By means of this technique, Sender is able to retain all the expressive and evocative elements which give direct speech its flavour - questions, exclamations, interjections and the like - while giving the narrative a clear experiential focus as a series of events perceived and remembered by one person. He is thus able to combine in his narrative the verisimilitude and direct impact of an autobiographical account with the firm authorial control of an omniscient third-person narrative. References to the act of memory, normally taking the form of 'Recordaba Mosén Millán...', constitute the autobiographical frame which encloses the omniscient third-person narrative.

At times, however, Sender's flexible fusion of two narrative modes - autobiographical account and omniscient third-person narrative - leads to some authorial inconsistencies. For example, the scene in which Mosén Millán and Paco go to visit the dying peasant who lives in the caves on the outskirts of the village, in order to give him the Last Rites, is followed some pages later by the sentence: 'Veintitrés años después, Mosén Millán recordaba aquellos hechos' (p. 41). Firstly, we should note that the reference here to 'veintitrés años' is a slip of the pen as Raymond Skyrme has pointed out, since this would mean that Paco was only three years old when he went to the caves, but this event clearly took place after his first communion (*38*, p. 118). But, quite apart from this, it is clearly impossible for the priest to have recalled all the events subsequently described since he was present at only the first episode (the visit to the cave of the dying peasant). Only the omniscient narrator can have been aware of the subsequent scene in which Paco's father forbids his son from taking part in any further sacramental activities, and La Jerónima's exaggerated account of what ensued. Indeed, since a further dimension has been added to the account, namely, La Jerónima's story about Paco's father reprimanding Mosén Millán for taking his son to the caves (p. 41), which Mosén Millán would presumably have been able to deny, then it is surely at points like these that the distinction between an autobiographical account and an omniscient third-person narrative is crucial. The narrator's ability to act at once as an omniscient impartial observer and as a reliable transcriber of Mosén Millán's subjective thoughts is thus fraught with technical problems.

We should not, however, fall into the trap of treating *Réquiem* as a disguised autobiographical work. This is clear if we examine more carefully the role that autobiographical structures play within the text. Paco's visit to the caves with Mosén Millán is the best example since this event, as Sender has admitted to Peñuelas, was based on a similar experience that he had as a young boy (*17*, pp. 199-200). Likewise, since the events described in *Réquiem* take place within an unnamed village in Aragon, a region where Sender spent much of his life, it is reasonable to speculate that some of the characters, events and customs which appear in the novel may be based on his own experience. It would be misguided, however, simply to see this novel, or indeed other novels by Sender, as fictionalized autobiographies. An attempt has, in fact, been made to produce a biography of Sender the man based on his fiction, with dubious results. Charles L. King has pointed to some of the dangers of this type of bio-literary approach (*13*, p. 16). Some incidents in the novel, for example, are clearly not based at all on lived experience. Whereas in the novel Paco moves away from the church and becomes interested in politics, thereby following his father's footsteps, Sender's own relationship with his father was diametrically opposed. Sender's father was a very religious man against whom the novelist rebelled at a very early age, as one of his childhood friends, Antonio Sierra, remembers (*13*, p. 16). In this particular instance, fiction and fact are at the farthest remove from each other.

Another distinctive characteristic of Sender's realism is evident in the way the novel articulates the space-time continuum. For, whereas the typical nineteenth-century realist text always clarifies its own spatial and temporal parameters, Sender's novel is curiously reticent on this point *(37*, p. 73). While we can be sure that Galdós's novel *Fortunata y Jacinta* is set in Madrid during the Restoration Period, *Réquiem* does not provide the reader with this kind of information.[3] There is a variety of reasons for this which I shall discuss later, but let us first address the problem of what information the text provides about its spatial and temporal parameters. While the village is unnamed throughout, the mention in the text of the village as 'cerca de la raya de Lérida' (p. 14) gives it clearer geographical co-ordinates. It is almost certain that the 'capital de provincia' to which don Valeriano and don Gumersindo retreat after the controversial land reforms are implemented, though unnamed, is Lérida (p. 79). As for the temporal co-ordinates, these can be deduced in a similar manner. Since the Requiem Mass is held a year after Paco's execution, which took place soon after the outbreak of the Civil War, then we must assume that the Mass is taking place in the summer of 1937 ('Un año después Mosén Millán recordaba aquellos episodios', p. 91). Paco's baptism occurred 26 years before ('Veintiséis años después se acordaba de aquellos perdices...', p. 17), namely in 1911. He was confirmed in 1918 ('Tenía Paco siete años cuando llegó el obispo, y confirmó a los chicos de la aldea', p. 27). Paco married Agueda in the spring of 1931, three weeks before the municipal elections, which took place on 12 April 1931 and in which socialists and middle-class republicans swept the board ('Tres semanas después de la boda volvieron Paco y su mujer, y el domingo siguiente se celebraron elecciones', p. 67). Reference is made obliquely to Alfonso XIII's abdication which also took place in April 1931, although Sender's

[3]See Stephen M. Hart, 'Galdós's *Fortunata y Jacinta:* An 'Inoffensive Hen'?', *Forum for Modern Language Studies*, 22 (1986), 342-53 (pp. 342-44).

text is elliptic: 'Se supo de pronto que el rey había huido de
España' (p. 67). Paco is executed about a fortnight after the
outbreak of the Civil War (18 July 1936); we may remember that,
when he is dragged from his hiding-place, Mosén Millán notices he
has a 'barba de quince días' (p. 98). It should be pointed out,
however, that there are two examples in the text when the
chronology is deficient. These are the references to 'siete años
después' (p. 63) and 'veintitrés años después' (p. 41), which are, as
Raymond Skyrme has argued, almost certainly slips of the pen (*38*).
It is possible, however, that Sender has deliberately introduced
inconsistencies of this kind in order to underline the fallibility of
Mosén Millán's memory, as Emiliano Luna Martín has pointed out
(*33*).

Other events, though probably not based on any specific
instance, were common enough for us to regard them as historically
valid. One example is Paco's suppression of the 'bienes de señorío'
(p. 70), around which there was fierce controversy during the
turbulent years of the Second Republic. During that period, the
Socialist Ministers of Labour, Francisco Largo Caballero, and of
Justice, Fernando de los Ríos, issued a series of decrees designed to
improve the lot of farm labourers. The imbalance in rural leases
which favoured the landlords was rectified. Eviction was made
almost impossible, rent rises were blocked while prices were
falling, and the eight-hour day was introduced (*8*, p. 21). Yet, even
here, Sender's narrative is not, strictly speaking, historically
accurate. As Skyrme has pointed out: 'The Agrarian Law which
Paco invokes in support of his case against the Duke applied only in
Andalusia, Estremadura, three provinces of Castile and Albacete in
Murcia, while that area of the province 'cerca de la raya de Lérida',
in which the novel is set did not support the insurgency, and
remained Republican until the Nationalist push to the
Mediterranean in the spring and summer of 1938' (*38*, p. 120).
Sender clearly wished to conjure up the atmosphere of political
strife characteristic of the years of the Second Republic, without
worrying overmuch about historical accuracy. Another event which
springs to mind is the clandestine noctural execution during the

Civil War of political undesirables in the Republican as well as the
Nationalist zone, which is alluded to succinctly and vividly in
Sender's text (p. 84), and attested by numerous accounts.[4]

Yet, if there are so many events and customs which are based
on generalized historical experience, then, why, we may
legitimately ask, does Sender not provide us with more concrete
details? Why are the village, Paco's father (simply referred to as 'el
padre de Paco'), the shoemaker ('el zapatero'), the bishop ('el
obispo'), the Duke ('el duque'), King Alfonso XIII ('el rey'), the
Nationalist officer ('el centurión') not given a name? There are
probably two reasons for this. Firstly, as Charles L. King has
argued, Sender wished to shroud his own life with a sense of
mystery, in order to protect his inner life from the prying eyes of
others (*13*, p. 14). Secondly, and more importantly, Sender wished
to universalize the experience of how the Civil War disrupted the
everyday life of a small village. By avoiding giving names to many
of the characters, or giving them generic names, he is able to
transcend the *costumbrista* mode and produce a work which is
relevant to all parts of Spain. A good example of this is the
masterful depiction of how some people arrive in the village, beat
up the shoemaker and kill six of the peasants from the caves. The
whole village is shocked and bewildered by their actions. No-one
knows who they are. They are simply referred to as 'señoritos
forasteros' (pp. 80-81).

One other aspect of the narrative further problematizes its
status as apparently translucent realism. Robert G. Havard shows
that there is textual interference between the ballad and the third-
person narrative of Paco's life, which ultimately recharges
'language-style, structure and theme with its own ancient and
traditional values' (*30*, p. 96). This is mainly evident, Havard
argues, in the use of numbers and repetition in the narrative in order
to capture the traditional mode and spirit of story-telling. We see a

---

[4]See *8*, p. 104, and p. 122. José María Gironella's novel *Un millón de
muertos*, 5th ed. (Barcelona: Planeta, 1962), pp. 139-40, also gives a
graphic reconstruction of events of this kind. See also Juan Benet,
Volverás a región, 2nd ed. (Barcelona: Destino, 1984), p. 186.

similar process of criss-crossing between the two levels in the use
of names and epithets. Paco, for example, is invariably referred to
as Paco el del Molino, showing how the language of the ballad
gradually invades the narrative of the real. Similarly, the
Nationalist officer is never given a name, but simply referred to as
'el centurión'. Awareness of the anomaly of this term surfaces in
the text through the words of the altar-boy, who quotes two lines
from the ballad '...y al llegar frente a las tapias / el centurión echa
el alto', and then comments: 'Eso del centurión le parecía al
monaguillo más bien cosa de Semana Santa y de los pasos de la
oración del huerto' (p. 12). This reference reinforces the biblical
allusiveness of the account of Paco's death. A further example of
the intrusion of the ballad's imagery into the narrative is the
fleeting and poetically-charged reference to the young girl who is
saddened by the wedding between Paco and Agueda: 'Una mozuela
decía viendo pasar la boda, con un cántaro en el anca: - ¡Todos se
casan, y yo, mira!' (p. 55). As she utters her jealous words and with
her water-jug resting on her hip, this young girl has a stylized,
literary poise about her. It is almost as if a literary image extracted
from the world of Spanish ballads had suddenly materialized in the
prose of everyday life, to produce what Scott Johnson has called
'lyric realism' (*3*, p. 28). But perhaps the most striking example of
catalystic interference between the two levels of reality and myth is
the description of the mischievous behaviour of the church icons
when Paco's colt is found in the church: 'Seguían acosando el
animal. En una verja - la de la capilla del Cristo - un diablo de forja
parecía hacer guiños. San Juan en su hornacina alzaba el dedo y
mostraba la rodilla desnuda y femenina' (p. 94). Fantasy and reality
become as one, as the mythic story-telling devices of the ballad
invade the narrative.

2. Characterization

Paco El Del Molino ~~a revolutionary~~ deemed a criminal.

Paco, the 'personificación simbólica del campesino español', as Peñuelas suggests (*18*, p. 151), is the hero of Sender's novel, since he is the man who fights for the rights of the underprivileged in society, and who eventually suffers death because of his beliefs. Like all the revolutionaries that people Sender's narratives Paco is *his crime is idealism* an idealist, as Rosario Losada Jávega points out (*14*, p.10). Paco's life, however, also has an archetypal structure since, as Peter A. Bly shows, it is 'the story of Man's life on earth: a succession of surprises and enigmas that with time are resolved by the ultimate betrayal of death' (*23*, p. 99). What makes Paco's fate so poignant is that he is betrayed by his spiritual father, Mosén Millán. As the priest muses to himself early on in the narrative, everyone liked Paco, except don Valeriano and don Gumersindo. Even as a child, Paco was clearly an attractive person. Mosén Millán took a deliberate interest in his spiritual welfare; the bishop who visited the village in order to confirm Paco was also obviously impressed by him (p. 27). A precocious child, Paco was moved by the mysteries of Holy Week (pp. 30-31). But perhaps most distinctive about Paco was his perceptiveness and intelligence. His answer to Mosén Millán, when questioned about the pistol he kept hidden under his clothes, that he kept it himself in order to prevent other naughtier boys from using it, leaves the priest dumbfounded (p. 27). Equally piercing are his questions and observations on the subject of the visit to the caves to administer the Last Rites to a dying peasant: 'Se está muriendo porque no puede respirar. Y ahora nos vamos, y se queda allí solo' (p. 38). His attitude towards poverty is down-to-earth and makes Mosén Millán's piety seem shallow. Talking of the couple's son, supposedly in prison, Paco comments:

> - Su hijo no debe ser muy malo, padre Millán.
> - ¿Por qué? - Si fuera malo, sus padres tendrían dinero.
> Robaría. (p. 39)

The visit to the caves is in fact crucial to Paco's growth in social awareness. He comes to realize that the Church has nothing to offer to alleviate the sufferings of the poor (*36*, pp. 114-15). This episode was based, as mentioned above (p. 16), on an experience Sender had as a seven-year-old child, which changed his life. As he pointed out to Peñuelas, 'fui desde entonces un ciudadano discrepante y una especie de escritor a contrapelo ... No necesitaba como base para la protesta ningún libro de Bakunin, ni de Marx, o de Engels, aunque los leyera más tarde. Estaba convencido desde niño' (*17*, p. 200). Paco, from this point onwards, gradually moves further and further away from the Church. His emancipation from Mosén Millán's spiritual authority takes two complementary forms. Firstly, it takes the form of sexual liberation when Paco swims nude in front of the washerwomen at the 'plaza de aguas' (pp. 43-44). As Laureano Bonet argues, Paco swimming in the water is a 'nuevo bautizo, ahora erótico' (*15*, p. 441). Secondly, he moves away from the Church through his growing political activism. He begins to question the Duke's right to demand rent from the farmers who plough his land: 'Paco creía que aquello no era cabal' (p. 44). His liberation from the Church is complete when he refuses, against his mother's advice, to take part in the Penitential Procession during Holy Week.

One specific event which takes place at this particular juncture in the novel demonstrates Paco's single-minded determination where social justice is concerned. He ignores the mayor's prohibition of 'rondallas', and goes ahead with one. When challenged by two policemen, he takes away their guns (p. 52). Perhaps even more significant is his reaction when he is reprimanded for this action by Mosén Millán. He states that he would prefer to rid the village of the social deprivation suffered by those living in the caves rather than have a police force. This shows quite clearly that Paco, even as an adolescent, sees social deprivation as caused by authoritarian repression, in other words as a political reality, rather than a God-given state of affairs (which is essentially Mosén Millán's view). This incident marks the beginning of a rift between the priest and Paco. David Henn has pointed out that, as Paco's political commitment deepens, 'the priest moves gradually from affection toward Paco to resentment and at times even hostility, until he is ultimately instrumental in the destruction of the peasant' (*31*, p. 108).

Paco has in effect cut all ties with the Church when he sees eye to eye with his father and realizes the value of politics as a means of achieving social change:

> El padre de Paco vio de pronto que todos los que con él habían sido elegidos se consideraban contrarios al duque y echaban roncas contra el sistema de arrendamientos de pastas. Al saber esto Paco el del Molino, se sintió feliz, y creyó por vez primera que la política valía para algo. 'Vamos a quitarle la hierba al duque', repetía. (pp. 67-68)

When questioned by Mosén Millán about his political activism, Paco refers specifically to the visit they both made to the caves as the event which forged his political destiny:

> - Diga la verdad, Mosén Millán. Desde aquel día que fuimos a la cueva a llevar el santolio sabe usted que yo y otros cavilamos para remediar esa vergüenza. Y más ahora que se ha presentado la ocasión.
> - ¿Qué ocasión? Eso se hace con dinero. ¿De dónde vais a sacarlo?
> - Del duque. Parece que a los duques les ha llegado su San Martín. (p. 68)[5]

---

[5]San Martín is traditionally the season for slaughtering pigs, and the phrase 'llegar su San Martín' has come colloquially to connote an

True to his words, once Paco is elected to the local council, he begins implementing wide-ranging rural reforms designed to better the lot of the peasants living in the caves. He informs don Valeriano that no rent will be paid to the Duke until a decision about the 'bienes de señorío' is made. When the Duke issues a 'shoot on sight' threat to anybody trespassing on his land, Paco cleverly outmanoeuvres him by having his guards offered better-paid work elsewhere. Though only recently elected to office, Paco is already an astute politician.

Paco also has the courage and conviction of his own ideals. In his interview with don Valeriano, he refuses to budge from his position. As he says to don Valeriano: 'No hay que negociar, sino bajar la cabeza' (p. 73). One further important quality of Paco's character is the way he trusts other people. He trusts the peasants who live in the caves, unlike Mosén Millán (pp. 52-53). This is in a sense his tragic flaw, for it leads him to trust Mosén Millán, just as his father had done before him by revealing his son's hiding-place. Paco accepts the priest's promise that no harm will come to him if he surrenders to the Nationalist army. It is only when he is being led out to execution that he fully realizes that he has been betrayed by his spiritual father:

- En mala hora lo veo a usted - dijo al cura con una voz que Mosén Millán no le había oído nunca. Pero usted me conoce, Mosén Millán. Usted sabe quién soy. (p. 99)

It is at the point of death that Paco's Christ-like status becomes most evident. Cedric Busette has argued forcefully that he is a Christ-like figure, since, although he dies physically, 'his spirit must forever haunt the conscience of Spain as the unrealized possibility of rebirth' (*25*, p. 486). Certainly, there are many indications to this effect, especially in the closing pages of the novel. The most obvious allusion is the description of the Nationalist officer as 'el centurión', thereby pointing to the biblical

individual's impending doom. The last sentence of the extract has the rough meaning of: 'It looks like the Dukes' time has (finally) come.'

centurion who is instructed by Pontius Pilate to crucify Christ and who exclaims, 'Truly this man was the Son of God', after seeing the manner of Christ's death (Mark 15:39). Sender's 'centurión', however, does not feel remorse for his action after executing Paco. Pointing in a similar direction is the fact that Paco is executed along with two other men, strongly recalling the biblical narrative in which Christ is described as crucified alongside two thieves (Mark 15:27). Mosén Millán specifically refers to Christ in the final confession scene, although he fails to appreciate fully his role in Paco's betrayal: 'A veces, hijo mío, Dios permite que muera un inocente. Lo permitió de su propio Hijo, que era más inocente que vosotros tres' (p. 100). Paco is stunned by these words, since he suddenly realises that Mosén Millán is quite prepared to allow him to be sacrificed as a propitiatory victim. Three other factors seem to suggest Paco's Christ-like status. Firstly, as M.A. Compitello argues, the use of precisely twelve snatches of ballad to describe Paco's life is reminiscent of the twelve stations of the Cross (*26*, p. 96, n. 14). A second factor tending to underscore the intertextual link between the life of Paco and the life of Christ is Paco's altruism in the face of death (he seems more concerned about his family and the other two convicts than himself). A third factor pointing in the same direction is Paco's spiritual innocence - hence his inability to understand the priest's question about whether he repents of his sins: 'Era la primera expresión del cura que no entendía' (p. 101). This tends to suggest that Paco was without sin when he died.

In a sense, like Christ, Paco does demonstrate a type of resurrection since, most critics agree, he returns in the guise of his colt which interrupts the Requiem Mass by mysteriously entering the church. The colt had been mentioned on the first page of the narrative: 'Más lejos, hacia la plaza, relinchaba un potro. '"Ese debe ser - pensó Mosén Millán - el potro de Paco el del Molino, que anda, como siempre, suelto por el pueblo"' (p. 1). The entrance of the colt into the church later on, as Charles L. King argues, represents 'the mute and animal-like protest of the people against the crime committed against Paco, who comes to be not only an individual but to symbolize the people themselves' (*13*, p. 77). The colt tends to suggest that the values of the people, which are symbolised by Paco, are eternal, as Eduardo Godoy Gallardo argues (*15*, p. 431). Sender himself confirms this view when he states in an interview with Peñuelas that, despite being a victim, Paco symbolizes the immortality of the people: 'El pueblo español es inmortal, como son todos los pueblos. Su proyección hacia el futuro es inmensa' (*17*, p. 131).

Mósen Millán

If Paco is a Christ-like figure, then Mosén Millán can be seen as representing the figure of Judas, for he is the person who has Paco's trust and yet betrays him. The only explicit reference to Judas in the novel, however, is to the 'beso de Judas' which is one of the elements which so impresses Paco during Holy Week as a young boy (p. 33). The whole narrative which reconstructs Paco's life expresses Mosén Millán's vain attempt to expiate his own sins. His guilt is, perhaps, most clearly suggested by the fact that none of the villagers attends the Requiem Mass, and also by the fact that he is the only other person named in the ballad apart from Paco; he appears as 'Mosén Millán el nombrado':

> aquel que lo bautizara,
> Mosén Millán el nombrado,
> en confesión desde el coche
> le escuchaba los pecados. (p. 65)

We also hear, significantly, how sensitive Mosén Millán is to these particular lines of the ballad; 'quería evitar que el monaguillo dijera la parte del romance en la que se hablaba de él' (p. 65). He sends the boy out on an errand, and, as Havard argues, the accusation of his guilt is 'all the more poignant for the lines' being remembered by the priest in silence' (*30*, p. 90). This reference to 'Mosén Millán el nombrado' is all the more pointed if we consider that many of the characters in *Réquiem* are unnamed (see Chapter 1).

It is clear right from the beginning of the narrative that Mosén Millán sees his priesthood in purely ritual terms. Even the Requiem Mass itself, as David Henn has pointed out, 'ostensibly an act of contrition is, in reality, merely another mechanical act, another Church ritual which serves to emphasize the priest's limitation as a man who is able to administer the rites of his religion but who has lost sight of its spirit and goals' (*31*, p. 111). While Mosén Millán is prepared to administer the Last Rites to the dying peasant in the caves, he feels no Christian compassion for the plight of others. He simply says of the dying man, 'Dios lo acoja en su seno' (p. 36), restricting his Christian duty to a purely ritualistic level. This scene, as we have seen, becomes the event which sows the seeds of Paco's future political commitment. Yet this scene is also crucial to an understanding of Mosén Millán's attitude towards Paco.

Mosén Millán's dominance of every aspect of Paco's life surfaces involuntarily during his speech many years later at Paco's wedding, which he concludes with the following words: 'Este humilde ministro del Señor ha bendecido vuestro lecho natal, bendice en este momento vuestro lecho nupcial - hizo en el aire la señal de la cruz - y bendecirá vuestro lecho mortal, si Dios lo dispone así' (p. 54). As it turns out, Mosén Millán's reference to blessing Paco's death-bed is a grim foreboding. It is significant that, apart from finding Mosén Millán's reference to his death-bed inappropriate, Paco should immediately be reminded of the same scene in which he visited the old dying peasant in the cave. This episode shows that Mosén Millán feels no compunction about playing God with other people's lives, while at the same time consistently failing to fulfil his priestly duty as the Vicar of Christ's love on earth. Mosén Millán is, indeed, often depicted as a 'minister of death' (*35*, p. 55). We have already seen that Paco takes on a Christ-like status at the point of death; and it is not coincidental that the dying peasant in the cave should also have been associated with the crucified Christ: 'Además el enfermo tenía los pies de madera como los de los crucifijos rotos y abandonados en el desván' (p. 39). Yet Mosén Millán was unable to see this, and thus failed to carry out his Christian duty of serving Christ in

others. As if to make the parallel between the dying peasant and
Paco all the more compelling, it is significant that, during each
incident when Mosén Millán administers the Last Rites, he takes an
altar-boy along with him. The altar-boy who is helping Mosén
Millán organize the present Requiem Mass in 1937 had, indeed,
witnessed Paco's execution:

> Eso de llorar no era verdad, porque el monaguillo vio a
> Paco, y no lloraba. 'Lo vi - se decía - con los otros
> desde el coche del señor Cástulo, y yo llevaba la bolsa
> para que Mosén Millán les pusiera a los muertos el
> santolio en el pie.' (p. 11)

The fact that Paco, as an altar-boy, should witness Mosén Millán
administering the Last Rites to a person for whom he feels no
compassion, and that he one day should find himself in a similar
position to that person, gives a grim sense of inevitability and
predestination to the narrative.

The episode in which Mosén Millán and Paco visit the dying
peasant is also crucial for a further reason. Firstly, Mosén Millán
fails to bring the light of the gospel to the home of the dying man.
It is surely not coincidental that the expression 'no había luz' is
repeated twice in this passage (pp. 35, 36). Mosén Millán's actions
thus become a grim parody of the statement in the Beatitudes that
Christians 'are the light of the world' (Matthew 5:14). Closely
associated with Mosén Millán's failure to bring light to others is his
own recognition that he is no longer 'the salt of the earth': 'Era
viejo, y estaba llegando - se decía - a esa edad en que la sal ha
perdido su sabor, como dice la Biblia' (p. 12). The citation is once
more based on the Beatitudes: 'You are salt of the earth; but if salt
has lost its taste, how shall its saltness be restored?' (Matthew
5:13). Secondly, in the course of his discussion with Paco as they
walk back to the village from the caves, Mosén Millán shows his
true Christian colours when probed by Paco's perceptive questions.
His reaction to Paco's concern about others is to resort to an
unquestioning fatalism; 'La vida es así y Dios que la ha hecho sabe

por qué', and later: 'Cuando Dios permite la pobreza y el dolor ... es por algo' (p. 39). He attempts to sweep aside as irrelevant the issue of human poverty in their village by insisting that there are worse-off people elsewhere: 'Esas cuevas que has visto son miserables pero las hay peores en otros pueblos' (p. 40). He repeats the same idea to Paco, this time angrily, when Paco questions the Duke's right to demand rent from the villagers (pp. 44-45). Mosén Millán clearly has no time for notions of social justice or social equality. When the Nationalist army kill some of those who lived in the caves, the priest simply complains not about murder, but about the fact that they were not given the Last Rites before execution (p. 88). The superficiality of Mosén Millán's Christian vocation is suggested by the perfunctory way in which he repeats his prayers: 'Cincuenta y un años repitiendo aquellas oraciones habían creado un automatismo que le permitía poner el pensamiento en otra parte sin dejar de rezar' (p. 10).

Mosén Millán, without doubt, is a symbol of the Spanish Church. The name 'mosén' is a title traditionally given to the clergy in Aragon and Catalonia, as Angel Iglesias Ovejero has pointed out (*32*, p. 228). Sender's own view of the Church is, not surprisingly, generally hostile. In 1955 the Aragonese writer referred to the Spanish Church as 'la más cerril y obtusa de la humanidad' (*39*, p. 34). It is interesting to note, however, that this view contrasts sharply with his more tactful reference to the role played by the Spanish Church during the Civil War in a lecture he gave at the Ateneo in Zaragoza in 1974, in which he referred to the way the Church 'a veces ha bendecido ejércitos que han ido a pelear contra otros ejércitos también bendecidos por la misma Iglesia, y han debido poner a Dios en situaciones muy difíciles' (*21*, p. 61). Be that as it may, Mosén Millán, as a symbol of the Church, is associated, throughout the novel, with the higher échelons of society, the Duke, don Valeriano, don Gumersindo, Cástulo Pérez, and the forces of reaction, symbolized by the Nationalist army. This is primarily suggested by the priest's surname, which is the same as that of the Nationalist Lieutenant-Colonel, José Millán Astray, a man of sinister physical appearance because of the loss of an eye and an arm in combat (*8*, p. 109). Mosén Millán thus symbolizes the reactionary historical forces of Spain. As Sender himself clarifies, Mosén Millán 'es la inercia de la historia y el peso de esa inercia' (*17*, p. 131). Mosén Millán, indeed, actualizes the historical inertia of the Church by staying inert in his chair in the sacristy for the span of the narrative.[6]

We must assume that it is because Mosén Millán's conservative political sympathies are common knowledge in the village that the shoemaker taunts him in 1931 with the news that the monarchy is about to be toppled: 'En Madrid, pintan bastos, señor cura' (p. 56). The priest's high social rank is suggested by his taking first position during the party after Paco's wedding. Sender is careful to point out that the wedding guests are placed around the bride and groom according to social rank (p. 59). This is confirmed, on the outbreak of the Civil War, by the fact that don Valeriano and Mosén Millán are seated 'en lugares de honor' (p. 87) during the Nationalist political rally which takes place in the town hall. Mosén Millán's elevated social rank is confirmed during the Requiem Mass he holds for Paco which only the three rich men of the village attend. The villagers boycott the event. Mosén Millán is seen as a traitor by the lower classes.

Perhaps the most damning feature of Mosén Millán's character is his complicity in Paco's execution. It might be argued that he was an unwitting agent in Paco's death. Josefa Rivas, for example, suggests that Mosén Millán was 'una víctima de su categoría social' (*19*, p. 113). Juan Luis Alborg sees him as a victim of circumstances (*1*, p. 53). Eduardo Godoy Gallardo, likewise, argues that Mosén Millán was duped by the Nationalist army, and that his main sin was that of trusting untrustworthy men (*15*, p.

---

[6]Mosén Millán's name may also be an ironic reference to Berceo's *Vida de San Millán* in which the saint appears in the sky, together with St James and a troop of celestial cavalry, to rout Fernán González's Moorish enemies. Given the religious-cum-military nature of San Millán's divine intervention, it is plausible that Sender is drawing an ironic comparison between Mosén Millán and his saintly namesake. I am indebted to Professor A.D. Deyermond for drawing my attention to this allusion.

431). This is certainly Mosén Millán's view, for as he says to Paco before the latter is executed, 'Me han engañado a mí también. ¿Qué puedo hacer?' (p. 100). Yet there are a number of facts which suggest that the priest was an accomplice, even if naive, in Paco's execution. For example, Mosén Millán's motives for carrying out the various actions which eventually lead to his death are obscure. Despite his apparent confusion at what has gripped the town after the outbreak of the war, Mosén Millán decides to go and see Paco's father. The text states baldly: 'Nadie más que el padre de Paco sabía dónde su hijo estaba. Mosén Millán fue a su casa' (p. 85). If his motive for doing so is obscure, his motives for giving to understand that he knows where Paco is hiding are even less clear. We read: 'Por uno de esos movimientos en los que la amistad tiene a veces necesidad de mostrarse meritoria, Mosén Millán dio la impresión de que sabía dónde estaba escondido Paco' (p. 85). Once he is privy to this information, Mosén Millán decides to test himself, by keeping his secret to himself. However, the temptation becomes too great: 'Y le gustaba, sin embargo, dar a entender que sabía dónde estaba escondido. De ese modo mostraba al alcalde que era capaz de nobleza y lealtad' (pp. 87-88). The 'centurión' finally extracts the information from the priest, by taking his pistol out of his belt and placing it on the table, which Mosén Millán interprets (probably correctly) as a veiled threat. We then witness the priest's reasoning which leads him to reveal Paco's hiding-place:

> Quizás de aquella respuesta dependiera la vida de Paco.
> Lo quería mucho, pero sus afectos no eran por el hombre en sí mismo, sino *por Dios*. Era el suyo un cariño por encima de la muerte y la vida. Y no podía mentir. (p. 89)

Mosén Millán's reasoning is specious. His excuse that he only loves Paco for God's sake ('por Dios') is a pretext. Sender has elsewhere argued that to love things not for their sake, but for God's sake, is blasphemous and indecent:

> Amar las cosas por ellas mismas y como son - que es lo
> que hace don Juan - es virtuoso. Amarlas 'por Dios'
> como manda la Iglesia es blasfemo, es soberbio. Es
> indecente. (*39*, p. 39)

Mosén Millán's action here is clearly culpable. After revealing
Paco's whereabouts, he makes the 'centurión' promise that he will
give Paco a fair trial, which he must know to be unlikely. If this is
not enough, what surely obliges us to see Mosén Millán as an
accomplice of the Nationalists is the fact that, later on, he persuades
Paco to give himself up, by making a pointed reference to the
vulnerability of his family:

> - Paco, en el nombre de lo que más quieras, de tu mujer,
> de tu madre. Entrégate.
> No contestaba nadie. Por fin se oyó otra vez la voz de
> Paco:
> - ¿Dónde están mis padres? ¿Y mi mujer?
> - ¿Dónde quieres que estén? En casa.
> - ¿No les ha pasado nada?
> - No, pero, si tú sigues así, ¿quién sabe lo que puede
> pasar? (p. 96)

The priest's emotional blackmail pays off, and Paco gives himself
up. When he emerges, Mosén Millán goes so far as to believe that
he has a guilty air about him: 'Viéndolo Mosén Millán le
encontraba un aire culpable' (p. 98). On the basis of his actions, we
must, therefore, surely see Mosén Millán as an accomplice of the
Nationalists. It is for this reason that Paco's final words, 'El me
denunció..., Mosén Millán, Mosén Millán...' ring through the
priest's mind for a long time after the event. Mosén Millán simply
feels disdain for those who have been executed in this summary
way: 'Pensando Mosén Millán en los campesinos muertos, en las
pobres mujeres del carasol, sentía una especie de desdén
involuntario, que al mismo tiempo le hacía avergonzarse y sentirse
culpable' (p. 103). Yet, even a year later, he cannot forget Paco's

Spanish

, as does society

death: 'La muerte de Paco estaba tan fresca, que Mosén Millán creía tener todavía manchas de sangre en sus vestidos' (p. 104). One positive point in Mosén Millán's favour is that he refuses to accept the money offered successively by don Valeriano, don Gumersindo and Cástulo Pérez. But this is a negligible virtuous act compared to his complicity in Paco's murder. The fact that Mosén Millán has not dared to take back Paco's belongings - his watch and his handkerchief - to his parents confirms the priest's guilt (p. 104).

The Three Rich Men

Don Valeriano, don Gumersindo and Cástulo Pérez are, in a sense, character types of rich men living in a rural village. This is no doubt inevitable given the brevity of Sender's narrative and the fact that they are secondary characters. We should perhaps remember that realism, despite its self-defining claim of empirical veracity, inevitably relies heavily on the use of types in the interests of economy.[7] All three of the men represent the sector of Spanish society which backed Franco's uprising. When Sender defined the main outline of his novel in the following terms, he clearly had these three men in mind: 'Es simplemente el esquema de toda la guerra civil nuestra, donde unas gentes que se consideraban revolucionarias lo único que hicieron fue defender los derechos feudales de una tradición ya periclitada en el resto del mundo' (*17*, p. 131). In their desire to defend the feudal rights of a outmoded social system, they each ally themselves with the Army and the Church. Yet despite their inevitable status as types these three characters are individualized in a subtle and convincing way. For each has consistent character traits which set them apart as individuals.

Of the three, don Valeriano is politically the most reactionary, being the Duke's administrator. He comments that those elected during the municipal elections are 'gente baja' (p. 67). Because of what he claims are illegal activities, he demands that the elections

---

[7]R. Wellek, 'The Concept of Realism in Literary Scholarship' (see note 1, above), pp. 240-41.

Army + Church + Aristocracy

be repeated (p. 70). After the elections, when his attempt to win over Paco fails, he retreats from the village to the capital of the province, and returns only when the Civil War breaks out. While he is prepared to donate an iron gate for the Christ Chapel in the parish church, his religious faith is linked to his political conservatism more than anything else. He argues, for example, during the years of the Republic, that a God who allowed such things to go on did not deserve so much respect (p. 77). There is some suggestion that he was actively involved in conspiring with the 'señoritos forasteros', since he is declared mayor of the village remarkably soon after the *coup* (p. 83). During the persecution he encourages the 'señoritos forasteros' to kill more people (p. 84).

Don Gumersindo is the least individualized of the three. Clearly not of don Valeriano's social rank, he is caricatured for his habit of repeating the phrase 'como el que dice', and for his constant references to his own kindness (p. 66). Cástulo Pérez, however, is, from a psychological point of view, more complex. While he is clearly rich, he decides not to cut his ties of allegiance with his 'class enemies'. Thus he attends Paco's wedding and offers to take the bride and groom to the train station in his car. This act of kindness surprises Mosén Millán who did not believe him to be such a good friend of the family (p. 59). Mosén Millán sees him as 'un carácter fuerte', eager to preserve his independence (p. 58). This is no doubt the reason why he is excluded from the private conversations held between don Valeriano, don Gumersindo and Mosén Millán shortly before the war (p. 80). Yet he is clearly an opportunist. After the outbreak of the war, he tells Mosén Millán that the Nationalists have machine-gunned the 'carasol' (p. 90), and he laughs, much to the priest's dismay. It is surely not coincidental that Cástulo Pérez should have brought the news and that his own wife should have been slandered only a short time before at the 'carasol' (see pp. 83-84). There is a suggestion, therefore, that Cástulo Pérez may have put the 'señoritos forasteros' up to the deed. He is also quite prepared to let his car be used for ferrying the priest over to the cemetery in order to administer the Last Rites to Paco, among others. He had offered the car for use by the new authorities (p. 99). The fact that his car is associated with Paco's marriage and his subsequent execution leads us to interpret the car, like Mosén Millán's wedding speech, as an allusive image of Paco's impending betrayal.

As a trio, these three men are united in their rejection of social equality and their adherence to a hierarchical social regime. In some ways, the fact that they each bring a gift to the Requiem Mass (they each offer in turn to pay Mosén Millán for the Mass), suggests that they are figures parodying the biblical narrative of the three wise men from the East with their gifts of gold, frankincense and myrrh (Matthew 2:1-12). The irony of their gesture is that, unlike the gifts of the three kings, theirs are nothing more than blood-money designed to appease their own consciences (*32*, p. 231).

The Shoemaker and La Jerónima

The shoemaker and La Jerónima are the two characters in the novel who, apart from Paco, are most opposed to Mosén Millán and the regime which he symbolizes. They represent what Sender elsewhere calls Spain's authentic, popular and illegal culture, which has been consistently repressed by social hierarchy.[8] The shoemaker is famous in the village for his anti-clerical sentiments. As he says to Paco one day:

> Los curas son la gente que se toma más trabajo en el mundo para no trabajar. Pero Mosén Millán es un santo.
>
> Esto último lo decía con una veneración exagerada para que nadie pudiera pensar que hablaba en serio. (p. 24)

Another witty jibe he makes against the clergy is that 'los curas son las únicas personas a quienes todo el mundo llama padre, menos sus hijos, que los llaman tíos' (p. 62). Despite the fact that he charges

---

[8]See Sender's article 'La cultura española en la ilegalidad', *Tensor* (August 1935); quoted in *12*, p. 181

Mosén Millán less to repair his shoes (p. 13), the priest is wary of
him and always addresses him formally using the 'usted' form.
When asked on one occasion by Mosén Millán whether he has been
to church, the shoemaker cannot conceal his anti-clerical
sentiments: 'Mire, Mosén Millán. Si aquello es la casa de Dios, yo
no merezco estar allí, y si no lo es, ¿para qué?' (p. 55). He taunts
Mosén Millán with rumours about the abdication of the King, but
when the Second Republic is declared, he becomes confused and
disoriented. It is at this point in the novel, indeed, that the villagers'
ability to communicate with each other 'now suddenly undergoes a
noticeable deterioration', as Peter A. Bly argues (*23*, p. 97). The
shoemaker's disorientation is thus symptomatic of the general
feeling of mental unease characterizing life during the troubled
years of the Republic. As a result of this, he refuses the post of
Irrigation Judge offered to him by the new authorities (p. 79). At
the outbreak of the Civil War, despite his neutrality, he is first of all
beaten up, and then murdered (pp. 81-82). He and La Jerónima are
great friends (and possibly also lovers); La Jerónima locks herself
in her house for three days when the shoemaker is found dead, not
least because she had mocked him the day before. He is murdered
because of rumours that he is a Russian agent (p. 83). Apart from
their anti-clericalism, the shoemaker and La Jerónima have one
other characteristic in common: their use of regional dialect. La
Jerónima, for example, uses regional expressions such as 'lechecita'
(p. 17), 'dijendas' (p. 19), 'saya de hierro' (p. 20), 'concencia' (p.
20), and 'patas puercas' (p. 84). But she is no match for the
shoemaker who greets her with news of the arrival of the Republic,
with the following string of abusive terms: 'Te lo digo a ti, zurrapa,
trotona, chirigaita, mochilera, trasgo, pendón, zancajo, pinchatripas,
ojisucia, mocarra, fuina...' (p. 63).

   Yet La Jerónima's rejection of the Church takes a specific
form which is distinct from the shoemaker's. She is, as Laureano
Bonet argues, the subconscious voice of the village, seen as
something separate from the Church (*15*, p. 441). Sender believed
the expression of the authentic voice of the people to be one of the
noblest tasks of the novelist, and, in the light of this, La Jerónima is

of crucial importance. As he declared in an interview with Peñuelas:

> Tal vez la tarea más útil del escritor, hoy por hoy,
> consista en aprender en el tumulto y caos de las
> multitudes la genuina voluntad y la voz auténtica del
> pueblo. Difícil y noble misión ésa. Es lo mejor que los
> escritores podemos tratar de hacer. (*16*, p. 206)

La Jerónima is associated throughout the narrative with gossip, sexual promiscuity and superstition. Her gossip, for which she has her own special word ('dijendas') takes a variety of forms. When reprimanded by the local doctor for touching Paco's umbilical cord, she attempts to persuade the young men in the village that the doctor has deliberately been paying visits on their wives when they are in a state of undress (pp. 20-21). She fabricates scandalous stories about the various crimes committed by those who take part in the Penitential Procession (p. 49). But normally her gossip is concerned with defaming Mosén Millán. She exaggerates the story about Paco's visit, with Mosén Millán, to the dying peasant in the cave, claiming that Paco's father said to the priest: ' ¿Quién es usted para llevarse al chico a dar la unción?' (p. 41). In the 'carasol', with which La Jerónima is closely associated, Paco's discussions with Mosén Millán and with don Valeriano are exaggerated to become full-scale threats (pp. 69-70). A hint of La Jerónima's sexual promiscuity is evident early on in the narrative from her comments about the size of Paco's 'atributos masculinos' after his baptism (p. 16). She boasts that she has had as many men as she wanted behind the church (p. 57).

Yet La Jerónima is most clearly singled out for her superstition. She is first referred to as 'partera y saludadora', and is known for her habit of leaving a pair of scissors under the pillow of a newly baptised boy to protect him from wounding by metal, or putting a rose previously dried in moonlight under a girl's pillow in order to make her beautiful and in order to protect her from difficult menstruations (p. 20). What is most striking about La Jerónima's type of superstition is that it takes its lead from superstitious Church customs. A good example of the innate superstition characterising ritual in the local church is the children's habit of beating strips of wood, reputed to contain Jews, when the priest pronounces the word 'resurrexit' during the Easter Vigil service (p. 33). Thus, La Jerónima used to add a Latin phrase to the end of the doxology when reciting the Lord's prayer which, in Mosén Millán's eyes, 'sonaba como una obscenidad' (p. 19). She would dance to the sound of church bells in the 'carasol' (p. 41); she had a remedy for soothing toothache which likewise incorporated church ritual: 'Mientras volteaban las campanas en la torre - después del silencio de tres días - la Jerónima cogía piedrecitas en la glera del río porque decía que poniéndoselas en la boca aliviarían el dolor de muelas' (p. 34). Rather than specifically rejecting the Church, La Jerónima grafts her own pagan rituals onto Christian customs.

It is significant that most of her activities take place in the 'carasol', for this is a type of space within the village community in which the secular rituals of rural life are enacted, in contradistinction to the Church, where the official life of the community takes place. Ironically, the word 'carasol' echoes the title of the Francoist hymn which the Nationalists are described as singing in the course of the novel, the 'Cara al sol' (*32*, p. 230). It is, moreover, not coincidental that the 'carasol' is associated, like the water square, with the sexuality repressed by the Church. It is at the 'plaza de aguas' that the young women, according to Mosén Millán, 'hablaban demasiado libremente' (p. 34). Young men, including Paco (for which he gets a reprimand from Mosén Millán), go there to swim in the nude. We read:

> Las lavanderas parecían escandalizarse, pero sólo de labios afuera. Sus gritos, sus risas y las frases que cambiaban con los mozos mientras en la alta torre crotoraban las cigüeñas, revelaban una alegría primitiva. (p. 44)

Likewise, much of the gossip which takes place at the 'carasol' centres on sexual matters. The women allude, for example, to Paco's wedding night 'con expresiones salaces' (p. 63). The 'carasol', like the 'plaza de agùas', is seen as a centre of political resistance against the church, for it symbolizes the natural, the rural and the sexual. It is no doubt because of its status as a focus for a quasi-pagan counterculture devoid of the values of officialdom that it is destroyed later on by the Nationalist army (p. 90; see *18*, p. 151). La Jerónima escapes being shot, and the last image we have of her is of a lonely figure driven mad by the experience of persecution:

> La Jerónima había vuelto a salir, e iba al carasol, ella sola, hablando para sí. En el carasol daba voces cuando creía que no podían oírla, y otras veces callaba y se ponía a contar en las rocas las huellas de las balas. (p. 104)

The 'carasol', the space formerly inhabited by popular culture, is evacuated of all meaning. Like La Jerónima, it is henceforth suppressed by officialdom as an anti-social and illegal madness.

3. Politics, Propaganda, and Style

Politics and Propaganda

One statement from Sender's posthumous *Toque de queda* (1985) perhaps best sums up his life-long interest in politics: 'Pertenezco a un partido que tiene un solo militante: yo. Así y todo discrepo y lo traiciono muchas veces cada día' (quoted in *10*, p. 91). His fiercely independent political stance, evident from this statement, emerged early on. As a young man in his twenties, he was deeply involved in left-wing politics. He had profound admiration for anarchists such as Ascaso, Durruti and Escartín, being a close friend of the last. He founded his own anarchist group called 'Espartaco' which had seven members, of whom he soon came to be the only survivor. True to his anarchist leanings, he regarded terrorism at that time as a valid political act. As he claimed in a conversation with Peñuelas: 'Yo creo que cuando un régimen es despótico, como la monarquía de entonces, el único recurso que queda es la acción violenta' (*17*, pp. 93-94). In 1927, Sender was imprisoned for three months for political activities (specifically, for attempting to overthrow the monarchy). From 1930 to 1932 he had a column entitled 'Postal política' in *Solidaridad obrera*, the daily newspaper of CNT (Confederación Nacional del Trabajo) (*16*, p. 14). In 1931 he became a member of CNT; he worked as a go-between within its organization, relaying messages between the Federación Local de Sindicatos de Madrid and the Confederación Regional de Cataluña. He also contributed to radical journals such as *La Libertad* and *El Socialista* (*10*, p. 36). He visited the Soviet Union in 1933, and he returned to Spain gushing with praise for the Soviet regime. As an open letter written in June 1933 and addressed to the International Union of Revolutionary Writers makes quite clear, Sender saw himself at that time as a revolutionary who had turned his back on his intellectual past and donned the uniform of 'un soldado del frente de lucha y de la edificación socialista' (*11*, p. 53). He later on worked for one year alongside the communists, although he did not at any time belong to a political party, believing the CNT to be more revolutionary than the Communist Party (*17*, p. 85). In the early months of the Civil War, Sender's wife and brother were executed by the Nationalist army. Sender asked to go to the Aragon front to fight alongside CNT troops, but his request was refused by the communists (*16*, p. 13). He eventually cut all ties with the communists shortly after the outbreak of the war, because of their Stalin-inspired persecution of members of the Trotskyist POUM (Partido Obrero de Unificación Marxista), many of whom were his friends. He later found out that he himself had been black-listed by Stalin (*17*, pp. 94-97). In December 1955 he wrote an angry letter from New York protesting that the journal *Ateneo* had referred to him as a communist (*15*, pp. 67-69). In an interview given to Peñuelas in the 1960s, Sender testified that his political ideas had become more moderate. He now believed in democratic socialism achieved by peaceful means (*17*, p. 201). Luz C. Watts quotes him as saying, in the 1970s, that he is a Christian anarchist (*21*, p. 14). As he sums up his political life in one of the pithy sayings of *Toque de queda:* 'Yo fui anarquista - extrema izquierda - luego filocomunista - extrema derecha - y finalmente como consecuencia de la desastrosa experiencia de la guerra civil, socialista fabiano, centro equilibrado' (quoted in *10*, p. 94).

Given a political pedigree of this kind, it is perhaps surprising that Sender should be unwilling to admit to any political influence in his literary writings. When questioned by Peñuelas, for example, he categorically denied that his work had political ramifications (*17*, p. 91). The reason for this assertion lies in the clear distinction he consistently draws between the aims of partisan politics and of art. Whereas 'lo político es lo que se puede referir a los intereses de un partido que busca el poder' (*17*, p. 91), the aim of art is something quite different: 'ampliar el radio de acción y el radio de visión de la naturaleza humana' (*17*, p. 178). Art thus transcends the desire to further the interests of any political party. Rather than expressing a predetermined point of view, it seeks to enhance and deepen our perception of human nature. Linked to this transcendence of a limited viewpoint is the stress Sender lays on lived experience in the novel form:

> Creo que ésa es la única virtud del novelista en lo cómico y en lo trágico. Una memoria selectiva un poco más fuerte de lo ordinario que organiza los materiales de la experiencia vital de uno, y los organiza de un modo instintivo, pero con una intención muy concreta y frecuentemente negativa. (*17*, p. 105)

In its emphasis on expanding the reader's perception of human nature and its reliance on lived experience (which is subsequently distilled carefully by the novelist's memory), Sender's novel is thus at the furthest remove from the *roman à thèse*.

In an interview with Peñuelas, Sender admitted that *Réquiem* possessed a very marked social dimension, but said that he did not have this in mind when he wrote the novel, which he saw mainly from an esthetic angle:

> No pensé en otra dimensión, sino en la expresión literaria directa de un problema en torno a una aldea. El problema tiene derivaciones sociales, que se desprenden solas como se desprende la neblina de un paisaje húmedo, esta vez húmedo de sangre. (*17*, p. 132)

Sender's emphasis on the esthetic rather than the political dimension of *Réquiem* may lead us to dismiss its political connotations as irrelevant. Certainly, a comparison between *Réquiem* and *Contraataque* (1938) might persuade us, at first glance, to underplay the political dimension of *Réquiem*. *Contraataque* is a record of Sender's experience as a volunteer officer at the Guadarrama and Madrid fronts during the first six months of the Civil War and, in this work, as Patricia McDermott has pointed out, there is 'a good deal of manipulation of material for the maximum propaganda effect' (*35*, p. 47). Catherine Belsey has defined propaganda as an 'imperative' type of literature which exhorts and instructs the reader, and Jacques Ellul argues that the aim of modern propaganda is 'no longer to modify ideas, but to provoke action'.[9] If one uses these yardstick definitions of propaganda, it is clear that *Contraataque* falls into this category, as McDermott stresses. This war diary is, as Michiko Nonoyama points out, anti-anarchist and pro-communist (*16*, pp. 34-37). *Réquiem*, however, is not a propagandistic work since it does not instruct the reader nor does it attempt to provoke political action of a clear-cut kind. At first glance, *Contraataque* and *Réquiem* seem to dovetail neatly with the evolution that Sender has pointed to within his own work. Since the war, he mentioned to Peñuelas, his work has progressed from being 'una literatura de combate inmediato' to being 'una literatura de iluminación' (*17*, p. 91). *Contraataque* seeks an immediate political effect, whereas *Réquiem* is concerned with esthetic enlightenment.

Yet while *Réquiem* is not propagandistic in a crude sense, it would be naive to deny that this 'intense and moving' work, as one critic calls it, has no political bias, for a connection between an author's political views and the art he produces is inevitable (see *2*, p. 75). Sender himself has stressed that the novel must inevitably have a social dimension (*17*, p. 19). He has also argued that the novel is 'un medio directo de expresión de la naturaleza del hombre. No del protagonista de la novela, sino de la naturaleza del autor. Porque en realidad todo lo que se pone en una novela lo extrae el autor de los elementos integrantes de su propia conciencia' (*17*, p. 171). These 'integrating factors' of the writer's conscience to which Sender here refers must also surely include political factors. How does this idea square with Sender's assertion that his own work does not have political ramifications?

---

[9]Catherine Belsey, *Critical Practice* (London: Methuen, 1980), p. 91; Jacques Ellul, *Propaganda: The Formation of Men's Attitudes*, translated by K. Kellen and J. Lerner (New York: Random House, 1973), p. 25.

George Orwell, as a result of his experience in Spain during the Civil War, became aware of a more subtle type of propaganda which is related to unconscious political prejudices. As he suggested in his memoirs: 'All art is to some extent propaganda ... Propaganda in some form or other lurks in every book ... Every work of art has a meaning and a purpose - a political, social and religious purpose.'[10] Thus even if we accept Sender's no doubt correct view that his art is not overtly political, it can be argued that it is inevitably aligned in a more subtle sense. As Raymond Williams has argued, 'writing, like other practices, is in an important sense always aligned, that is to say, that it variously expresses, explicitly or implicitly, specifically selected experience from a specific point of view'.[11] Yet how can we identify this political alignment in a work of literature which is not overtly political? The level at which political alignment is situated - the propaganda which 'lurks' in every work of literature, to use Orwell's phrase - is, as Terry Eagleton points out, within the work's unconscious ideological formation. Eagleton has defined ideological formation as a structure which is 'constituted by a relatively coherent set of beliefs which, realised in certain material apparatuses and related to the structures of material production, so reflect the experiential relations of individual subjects to their social conditions as to guarantee these misperceptions of the real which contribute to the production of the dominant social relations'.[12] Eagleton's reference to 'experiential' relations is crucial in this context, for in *Réquiem* we are presented with a politically aligned world-view as it emerges from the experience of a small number of the inhabitants of an Aragonese village during

---

[10]*Collected Essays, Journalism and Letters*, (Harmondsworth: Penguin, 1968), edited by Sonia Orwell and Ian Angus, II, pp. 152, 276; see also Zahir Jamal, 'Orwell in Spain', *Renaissance and Modern Studies*, XX (1976), 54-64.

[11]Williams, *Marxism and Literature* (Oxford: O.U.P., 1977), p. 199.

[12]*Criticism and Ideology. A Study in Marxist Literary Theory* (London: Methuen, 1976), p. 54.

the 1930s. This is, indeed, the key to the power of Sender's narrative.

The experience of the villagers is presented to us in what, at first sight, seems to be an objective account. Indeed, it could be argued that the charge of misrepresentation which might be levelled at Sender is forestalled since the narrative focus is provided by the local priest, who is, politically speaking, an enemy of the working class, and therefore unlikely to bias his report in favour of the villagers. Yet Sender uses this apparently unbiased narrative focus in order to point the finger at Mosén Millán and, by extension, at the Church for the role it played during the Civil War. Even if we accept the narrative as an objective account, blame is laid clearly at the door of Mosén Millán, the three rich men and the 'centurión de la cara bondadosa'. The centurion is prepared to lie to the priest in order to get his hands on Paco, whom he shoots summarily once he surrenders. Don Valeriano is described as encouraging the Nationalist troops to 'matar más gente' (p. 84); Cástulo Pérez probably encouraged the 'señoritos forasteros' to machine-gun the old women at the 'carasol' (see Chapter 2). Mosén Millán is, as we have seen, finally revealed as an accomplice of the Nationalists.

The Republicans, on the other hand, are saints in comparison. La Jerónima and the shoemaker are, at most, guilty of uttering anti-clerical witticisms; Paco's most heinous act seems to have been that of drinking, uninvited, don Valeriano's wine (pp. 74-76). The unjustified nature of this persecution is, perhaps, best exemplified by the putative motives behind the shoemaker's murder:

> - No es verdad - dijo alguien. Es porque el zapatero dicen que era agente de Rusia.
>
> Nadie sabía qué era la Rusia, y todos pensaban en la yegua roja de la tahona, a la que llamaban así. Pero aquello no tenía sentido. Tampoco lo tenía nada de lo que pasaba en el pueblo. (p. 83)

The absurdity of the idea that the shoemaker was a Russian agent is intended to demonstrate the irrational nature of the Nationalist purge. For a variety of reasons, thus, the dice are heavily loaded in the Republic's favour.

Sender's account is made all the more effective by his silence about uncomfortable historical facts. In his account of the Second Republic, for example, he refers to the Duke's threats when his land dues are threatened; but he declines to refer to the burning of churches by left-wing extremists during the same era (*8*, p. 23). As his journalism covering this historical period shows, Sender himself was in favour of more stringent agrarian reform, and did not reject church-burning. As he wrote: 'Si el pueblo incendia, hay que dejarle que incendie. Elimina naturalmente, siguiendo una sana ley biológica, lo que no debe existir' (quoted in *16*, pp. 18-19). In his novelistic account of the Civil War, equally, Sender refers to Nationalist, but not to Republican atrocities (*8*, p. 122). He is thus guilty of one of the most subtle ploys of propaganda, that is, *suppressio veri*.[13] Sender's indictment of the alliance of the Army, the Church and the landowners is made all the more effective by being presented through the eyes of the village priest. It is clear, therefore, that though *Réquiem* is not a propagandistic work, it is nevertheless, by virtue of the selection it makes of events depicted, politically aligned with the Republic.

Style

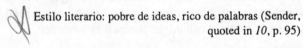

Estilo literario: pobre de ideas, rico de palabras (Sender,
quoted in *10*, p. 95)

This definition from Sender's *Toque de queda* perhaps best sums up his attitude towards style. 'Literary style', i.e. when mannered, is rich in words but poor in ideas. From this we may deduce that Sender's own preferred style is one that is not literary (if we

---

[13]See Michael Balfour, *Propaganda in War: 1939-1945* (London: Routledge and Kegan Paul, 1979), pp. 427-35. Sender's use of *suppressio veri* is mirrored in the narrative at those junctures when communication between individuals breaks down; see Peter A. Bly,*23*, and José Carlos Mainer, *34*, p. 128.

interpret the word to mean 'verbal affectation', as Sender clearly does here), but which is, conversely, rich in ideas and sparse in words. This, as we shall see, is certainly true of *Réquiem*. Sender saw style as the window onto a world-view rather than a combination of grammatical devices. As he wrote in an essay, 'Una manera de entender el estilo' (*La Libertad*, no. 4592, 19 December 1934): 'Hay en los libros grandes ventanas abiertas a sus almas, donde palpita y vive, fuerte, segura y distinta, una noción del universo capaz de fecundar las conciencias. Ese es el estilo' (quoted in *12*, p. 115).

Sender's style, at its most typical, is unadorned, concise and direct. He put great stress on the natural and spontaneous expression of one's ideas as opposed to rhetorical affectation. He points out, for example, in his prologue to *Los cinco libros de Ariadna:* 'Odio cualquier forma de afectación y me encanta en arte la simplicidad elaborada en la dirección de la naturaleza y no contra ella'.[14] As he suggested to Peñuelas in an interview:

> En realidad, el estilo surge espontáneamente del fondo del ser y, naturalmente, el mejor estilo es el que no se percibe. Cuando se percibe el estilo es que hay algo que interfiere entre el pensamiento del que escribe y la sensibilidad del que lee. Hay un escritor francés de principio de siglo que dice: cuando alguien en lugar de escribir 'un sou' escribe 'cinco céntimos', ya está atrapado por la retórica. (*17*, pp. 225-26)

Sender has indicated to Peñuelas that he retained a skill at writing concisely from his many years working as a journalist for *El Sol:*

> Tú sabes lo que es estar, como te digo, seis u ocho años no sólo escribiendo cada día, sino corrigiendo materiales que te enviaban a la mesa; que tú debías

---

[14]R.J. Sender, *Los cinco libros de Ariadna* (New York: Las Américas, 1957), p. xi.

limpiar de redundancias y de repeticiones y dejarlos
reducidos a la pura esencia informativa? Con lo cual
llega un momento en que has asimilado por lo menos
una virtud. La de discriminar y no decir sino cosas
interesantes. (*17*, pp. 106-07)

Sender's virtue - his ability to reduce a mass of information to its
essence - was based on his habit of writing a long first draft, and
then cutting it down to a more manageable size (*17*, p. 102). This
he often achieved by removing adjectives from the text:

Casi siempre cuando corrijo un texto, lo que hago es
quitar adjetivos. Porque la abundancia de adjetivos es
pobreza de expresión. Si suprimes los adjetivos y eres
tan expresivo como con ellos, el estilo cobra fuerza y
energía. (*17*, p. 230)

By consistently reducing his sentences to their 'pura esencia
informativa', Sender's style at times approaches the bare, simple
idiom described by Roland Barthes as the 'zero degree of
writing'.[15] Sender's emphasis upon concision and economy is
linked to his own liking for fast-moving plots, which no doubt
accounts for his admiration for Stendhal's novels (*17*, p. 226). Yet
by far the most important objective of Sender's style was that of
making the reality described in his novels believable. As he pointed
out to Peñuelas, the primary aim of the novelist is: 'hacer verosímil
la realidad' (*17*, p. 107). This did not always involve simply
copying life, since, as he has pointed out elsewhere, 'la vida misma,
fraccionaria o total, es escandalosamente inverosímil' (quoted in
10, p. 91; Sender gives an example of life's frequent lack of
verisimilitude in *17*, p. 220). Sender's emphasis on the virtue of
verisimilitude made him doubtful about the values of
experimentation with the novel form. He has, for example, harsh
words to say about the French *nouveau roman* and the Spanish-

---

[15]*Le Degré zéro de l'écriture* (Paris: Seuil, 1953).

American new novel (*17*, pp. 175-76 and 213; see, however, Carrasquer's view, *9*, p. 113).

The store Sender puts by concision and versimilitude is evident in his description of physical appearances. When he describes the physical appearance of the priest, for example, he refers only to those details which are functional and dramatic. There is no description for description's sake. In the opening scene of the novel, for instance, we are not informed as to what Mosén Millán looks like, what clothes he is wearing, his facial expression, etc. The reader is not privy to any of those kinds of detail which we should find in a nineteenth-century realist novel. We are simply told: 'El cura esperaba sentado en un sillón con la cabeza inclinada sobre la casulla de los oficios de réquiem' (p. 9). On the following page, we are given a few more details (the priest has his hands crossed on top of the chasuble, which is black and embroidered with gold; p. 10), but again, details which describe physical appearance are relatively few and far between. Sender's narrative is above all concerned with the dynamism of reality and the drama behind human gestures. In the extracts quoted, for example, the priest's posture suggests spiritual resignation and defeatism. Details involving physical descriptions are subordinated to the onward thrust of the plot, what Sender elsewhere calls the 'psicología del movimiento' (*10*, p. 91).

Throughout *Réquiem* there are, indeed, very few references to physical appearance. The physical appearance of not only Mosén Millán but also Paco is not elaborated upon. Sometimes, however, certain details are provided which act almost as epithets. Such is the case with the reference to La Jerónima's 'pata reumática' (p. 57), Cástulo Pérez's 'ojos fríos y escrutadores' (p. 58), don Valeriano with his 'bigotes, que estaban tan lamidos y redondeados, que parecían postizos' (p. 74), and 'el centurión de la cara bondadosa y las gafas oscuras' (p. 88). The longest description of physical appearance - lasting two sentences - is reserved, interestingly enough, for the bishop who visits the village in order to confirm Paco at the age of seven: 'La figura del prelado, que era un anciano de cabello blanco y alta estatura, impresionó a Paco. Con su mitra, su capa pluvial y el báculo dorado, daba al niño la idea aproximada de lo que debía ser Dios en los cielos' (pp. 27-28). But this is not typical. Sender normally keeps his description of physical appearance to a minimum.

Sender's verbal terseness is evident equally in his depiction of the characters' psychology. Here, he may have been influenced by the great classics of Spanish literature, such as *Poema de Mío Cid* and the *Quijote*, where analytical psychology of the type used in Balzac and Proust has no place (*17*, p.173). In *Réquiem*, except in the case of Mosén Millán, the reader must interpret characters' thoughts through an analysis of their words and actions, a device which Sender may well have perfected from his reading of novelists such as Hemingway and Faulkner whose work he admired (*17*, p. 213). Even in the case of Mosén Millán, the character's thoughts are reported without secondary comment, leaving once more the reader to draw his own conclusions. An example of this may be found in the opening pages of the novel where we might have expected the greatest amount of psychological detail to be introduced. Consider, for example, the following account of the priest's thoughts as he muses over whether the parishioners will attend the Requiem Mass:

> Esperaba que los parientes del difunto acudirían. Estaba seguro de que irían - no podían menos - tratándose de una misa de réquiem, aunque la decía sin que nadie se la hubiera encargado. También esperaba Mosén Millán que fueran los amigos del difunto. Pero esto hacía dudar al cura. (p. 10)

Mosén Millán's thoughts, which betray a mind racked by doubt about the role he played in Paco's execution, are presented in a matter-of-fact way without any embellishment. The priest's thoughts are not analysed; they are simply recounted. Sender's verbal economy leaves room for the reader to draw his own conclusions.

The distinctiveness of Sender's style is equally evident in his use of image. He stressed in an interview with Peñuelas that 'la palabra debe ser terriblemente funcional' (*17*, p. 231), and this is certainly the case with the rare images which appear in *Réquiem*. One example will suffice. On the first page of the novel, the priest is distracted momentarily from his thoughts by something he hears outside the sacristy window:

> Cerca de la ventana entreabierta un saltamontes atrapado entre las ramitas de un arbusto trataba de escapar, y se agitaba desesperadamente. Más lejos, hacia la plaza, relinchaba un potro. 'Ese debe ser - pensó Mosén Millán - el potro de Paco el del Molino, que anda, como siempre, suelto por el pueblo.' El cura seguía pensando que aquel potro, por las calles, era una alusión constante a Paco y al recuerdo de su desdicha. (pp. 9-10)

On a first reading, we may interpret the detail of the grasshopper caught in the branches of the shrub outside the sacristy window as purely naturalistic and incidental. Yet, through being juxtaposed with the subsequent reference to Paco's stray colt, the image of the grasshopper comes inevitably to symbolize Paco's death-trap of the year before. The second image, which associates Paco with his colt, is metonymic in that it 'shortens distances so as to facilitate the swift intuition of things already known'. Since this was the colt that Paco himself owned, we associate it naturally with him. During the course of the narrative, the colt acts as a substitute for Paco. The first image, which associates Paco with the trapped grasshopper, works in a more subtly allusive way. It is metaphoric in that it is a 'condensed comparison by which we assert an intuitive and concrete identity'.[16] Here it is the fact that Paco, like the

---

[16]The definitions of metonymy and metaphor are by G. Esnault. See Stephen Ullman, *Language and Style* (Oxford: Basil Blackwell, 1964), pp. 176-180. I.A. Richards has defined 'tenor' as the thing we are talking

grasshopper, was *trapped* within circumstances that were not of his own making that establishes the link between them. As we can see, the explicit metonymic association between Paco and the colt engenders a further intuitive link between Paco and the trapped grasshopper. While the vehicle is identical in each image (Paco), the tenor is different, although both are, significantly enough, drawn from the animal kingdom (grasshopper and colt). What at first sight seem to be naturalistic details turn out, on further analyis, to be highly functional images with symbolic undertones embedded within what Eugenio G. de Nora has called the 'equilibrada y clásica estructura' of Sender's novel (*4*, p. 45).[17]

---

about and 'vehicle' as that to which the tenor is compared; see the discussion in Ullman, *ib.*, pp. 184-93.

[17]For further discussion of the use of everyday objects with symbolic connotations in Sender's work, see Julia Uceda, 'Realismo y esencias en Ramón Sender', *Revista de Occidente*, 28 (1970), 39-53.

Conclusion

This short study of *Réquiem por un campesino español* has concentrated on four aspects of Sender's novel: plot, characterization, politics and style. In the section on plot, we have seen that Sender's narrative moves skilfully from the past, as reconstructed by Mosén Millán's memories, and the present, as the priest sits waiting in vain for his parishioners to attend the Requiem Mass. A link between these two temporal planes is provided by the ballad which recounts the life of Paco el del Molino and which periodically interrupts the flow of the priest's memories. Sender deliberately avoids specifying the temporal and spatial co-ordinates of the setting of the novel in order to universalize the experience depicted. In terms of its characterization, *Réquiem* clearly has recourse to the use of character types: Paco, for example, represents the Spanish people, Mosén Millán the Church, the shoemaker and La Jerónima anti-clericalism, and don Valeriano, don Gumersindo and Cástulo Pérez the landed gentry who backed Franco's crusade. The struggle between Mosén Millán and Paco, which intensifies as the plot progresses, reaches a climax as Paco is betrayed by the priest. Unlike the earlier *Contraataque*, which is also based on the Spanish Civil War, *Réquiem* is not a propagandistic work. However, an analysis of plot and characterization shows that the political bias of this work is already weighted in the Republic's favour. In the section on style, we saw that *Réquiem* is characterized by a terse, concise and direct expression. Sentences are reduced to their syntactic essence; images are highly functional. For a variety of reasons, therefore, *Réquiem* fully deserves its description by Peñuelas as 'la narración más depurada de Sender' (*18*, p. 137).

Appendix: *'Réquiem por un campesino español'*: The film version (1985)

Réquiem por un campesino español was released in a film version in 1985. The film, directed by Francesc Betriu, is on the whole a faithful recreation in the cinematographic medium of Sender's novel. It is for this reason, perhaps, that John Hopewell refers to the 'simplistic vision' of Betriu's film, which he furthermore characterizes as a 'left-wing film'.[18] At any rate, it is undeniable that, unlike Carlos Saura's version of Lorca's *Bodas de sangre* (1980), Betriu's film version of Sender's novel is relatively unexperimental, keeping very close to Sender's original text. The great majority of the dialogues, for example, are taken verbatim from the novel. The film version, however, does delete certain scenes from the novel and elaborate on others, and I intend to look briefly at these changes.

First, the deletions. These range from the image of the trapped grasshopper which appears at the beginning of the narrative and which, as I have argued in Chapter 3, stands as an allusive symbol of Paco's fate. Attention is focussed instead, during the opening scenes of the film, on the colt which is shown running around the village: clearly, here, an image of freedom. Other deletions are structurally and thematically significant. Whereas in the text Mosén Millán is shown as wheedling the information about Paco's whereabouts from Paco's father (pp. 85-86), in the film he hears this from Paco himself. This difference tends to diminish the priest's guilt, since he becomes less of an active colluder in Paco's downfall. Pointing in a similar direction are the visual references in the film to Mosén Millán's remorse. He is sullen and clearly

---

[18]*Out of the Past: Spanish Cinema after Franco* (London: British Film Institute, 1986), p. 174.

displeased by the three rich men who each offer to pay for the Requiem Mass. He is also shown as racked with remorse during the dramatic scene in the film when he gives the last sacraments to Paco. He is crying and visibly moved in the film, whereas the book is less forthcoming about his grief. (By contrast, the altar-boy is depicted in the film as expressionless and unmoved, with almost sinister overtones.) Likewise, more sympathy for Mosén Millán's plight is ensured by the fact he is treated more aggressively by the 'centurión' in the film version than in the novel. The 'centurión' shouts at him and repeatedly bangs the table. The novel is much less explicit about the pressure brought to bear on Mosén Millán, suggesting rather than the 'centurión' gets his way by insinuation rather than force (pp. 88-89). Events such as these tend to make Mosén Millán more of a sympathetic character than the book suggests. Whereas, in the film, we may tend to believe Mosén Millán when he tells Paco in this final scene 'Me han engañado a mí también', in the book we have more doubts about his sincerity.

Perhaps of most significance in the film are the additions made to the original script. Most of these additions are extensions of scenes which are traceable back to the original text. An example is the scene which occurs half-way through the film describing the merriment at a local *fiesta*. Paco predictably manages to outperform his contemporaries by climbing up the *cucaña* (slippery-pole) and claiming the prize of the turkey tied to the top. Paco subsequently invites Agueda to dance and the scene cuts dramatically to their marriage ceremony. Other scenes explore in an allusive manner episodes which are referred to only elliptically in Sender's text. An example of this is the point in the film when Paco offers the Duke's guards better-paid jobs in the Trade Union, in order to avoid a confrontation. In the film, we then see Paco leading a flock of sheep triumphantly into the Duke's property. The film subsequently cuts to a panoramic view of the land to which Paco has now laid claim, with all the concomitant connotations of freedom from repression.

Some additions are interesting in that they explore some of the latent symbolic motifs in the novel, an example being the revolver. The film follows the book in describing an incident when Paco, as an altar-boy, is caught by Mosén Millán with a toy revolver under his vestments (pp. 26-27). Yet the film, unlike the book, takes the allusiveness of this symbol one step further. Firstly, the film manages to make the revolver more significant thematically by building in another scene in which Paco and his friend are reprimanded for playing with the toy gun during a confirmation class. But perhaps more subtle, the revolver reappears at the end of the film; it is glimpsed briefly when Mosén Millán looks at Paco's watch and handkerchief which he had intended to return to his next of kin after the execution, but which he had been unable, until now, to give back. (The novel had simply referred to Paco's watch and handkerchief; p. 104.) The sight, in the film, of the toy revolver next to the watch and the handkerchief throws into vivid contrast the innocent world of Paco's childhood and the adult world into which he grew up, where guns are no longer toys but are used to murder others. As we can see, additions of this kind are not only consistent with the text but stand as imaginative recreations of Sender's original artistic purpose.

Bibliographical Note

Included in this bibliographical note are works directly relevant to the present study. For a more comprehensive bibliography, see Elizabeth Espadas, 'Ensayo de una bibliografía sobre la obra de Ramón J. Sender', *Papeles de Son Armadans*, no. 74 (1974), 231-82, and no. 78 (1975), 245-59, and her more recent annotated bibliographies in *9*, pp. 121-77, and *20*, pp. 227-87; along with Charles L. King, *Ramón J. Sender: An Annotated Bibliography* (Metuchen, N.J.: Scarecrow, 1976), and his updated 'A Partial Addendum (1975-1982) to *Ramón J. Sender: An Annotated Bibliography*', *Hispania* (U.S.), 66 (1983), 209-16, and his most recent bibliography in *20*, pp. 201-25.

GENERAL BACKGROUND

1. Juan Luis Alborg, *Hora actual de la novela española*, II (Madrid: Taurus, 1962). Sound overview of Sender's work (pp. 21-23), although little space is dedicated to *Réquiem*.
2. José Domingo, *La novela española del siglo XX*, II (Barcelona: Labor, 1973). Contains introductory section on Sender (pp. 71-76).
3. Scott Johnson, *The Hero and the Class Struggle in the Contemporary Spanish Novel* (New York: Gordon Press, 1977). Discusses the role of the proletariat in a selection of twentieth-century novels. Reviews the role of politics in Sender's work (pp. 28-37).
4. Eugenio C. de Nora, *La novela española contemporánea*, II (Madrid: Gredos, 1962). Section on Sender (pp. 35-48) gives a favourable overview of his work.
5. Emir Rodríguez Monegal, *Tres testigos españoles de la guerra civil* (Caracas: Monte Avila, 1971). Compares Sender's novels inspired by the Civil War (pp. 21-43) with those by Max Aub and Arturo Barea.
6. Gonzalo Sobejano, *Novela española de nuestro tiempo* (Madrid: Prensa Española, 1970). Chapter 2 (pp. 43-73) outlines usefully some of the major trends of the Spanish Civil War novel.

7. Darío Villanueva, *Estructura y tiempo reducido en la novela* (Valencia: Bello, 1977), p. 264. Section on *Réquiem* examines plot structures (pp. 264-69).

8. Paul Preston, *The Spanish Civil War* (London: Heinemann, 1986). Clear and well-argued study of historical background.

GENERAL CRITICAL WORKS ON SENDER

9. Francisco Carrasquer, *La verdad de Ramón J. Sender* (Madrid: Cinca, 1982). Compares Sender's work with that of Angel Samblancat and Felipe Alaiz, as well as collecting previously published essays. Contains full annotated bibliography by Elizabeth Espadas (pp. 121-77).

10. José Luis Castillo-Puche, *Ramón J. Sender: el distanciamiento del exilio* (Barcelona: Destino, 1985). A readable study of Sender's work which stresses his roots in journalism.

11. Patrick Collard, *Ramón J. Sender en los años 1930-36: sus ideas sobre la relación entre literatura y sociedad* (Ghent: University of Ghent, 1980). Comprehensive study of Sender's journalism during the 1930s.

12. ———, 'Las primeras reflexiones de Ramón Sender sobre el realismo', in *Actas del Sexto Congreso Internacional de Hispanistas celebrado en Toronto del 22 al 26 de agosto de 1977*, ed. Alan M. Gordon and Evelyn Rugg (Toronto: University of Toronto, 1980), pp. 179-182. Concentrates on Sender's theory of dialectical realism.

13. Charles L. King, *Ramón J. Sender*, Twayne's World Authors Series 307 (New York: Twayne, 1974). Contains basic background information.

14. Rosario Losada Jávega, *Algunos aspectos de la novela española en la emigración: Ramón J. Sender* (Barcelona: University of Barcelona, 1966). 24-page abstract of the author's unpublished thesis accepted at the University of Barcelona on 23 June 1964; discusses characters, ideology, language and style in Sender's work.

15. José Carlos Mainer (ed.), *Ramón J. Sender: in memoriam* (Zaragoza: Diputación General de Aragón, 1983). A helpful collection of some of the best essays on Sender's work to date. Reproduces *24* and *28* described below.

16. Michiko Nonoyama, *El anarquismo en las obras de Ramón J. Sender* (Madrid: Playor, 1979). A well-documented study, evaluating his journalism and a selection of his novels.

17. Marcelino C. Peñuelas, *Conversaciones con R J. Sender* (Madrid: E.M.E.S.A., 1969). An indispensable collection of interviews dealing with the writer's views on literature and politics.

18. ——, *La obra narrativa de Ramón J. Sender* (Madrid: Gredos, 1971). A sensible and comprehensive study of Sender's work.

19. Josefa Rivas, *El escritor y su senda: estudio crítico-literario sobre Ramón J. Sender* (México: Mexicanos Unidos, 1967). Chapter on *Réquiem* (pp. 105-14) argues that Sender depicts Mosén Millán sympathetically as a victim of circumstances beyond his control.

20. Mary S. Vásquez (ed.), *Homenaje a Ramón J. Sender* (Newark, Delaware: Juan de la Cuesta, 1987). A collection of important essays on various aspects of Sender's work. Contains 26 described below.

21. Luz C. Watts, *Veintiún días con Sender en España* (Barcelona: Destino, 1976). A running commentary on Sender's first visit back to Spain in 1974 after many years of exile. The author was a former student of Sender's.

STUDIES ON 'REQUIEM'

22. María Leonor Andreu, '*Réquiem por un campesino español* y *Crónica de una muerte anunciada:* convergencias', *Escritura* (Caracas), 10, nos. 19-20 (January-December 1985), 127-37. Analyses and contrasts time and structure in these two novels by Sender and Gabriel García Márquez respectively.

23. Peter A. Bly, 'A Confused Reality and its Presentation: Ramón Sender's *Réquiem por un campesino español*', *The International Fiction Review*, 5 (1978), 96-102. Analyses the breakdown of communication between individuals in the novel, which finally erupts into the violence of war.

24. Laureano Bonet, 'Ramón J. Sender, la neblina y el paisaje sangriento: una lectura de *Mosén Millán*', *Insula*, no. 424 (March 1982). Argues that La Jerónima is the unconscious voice of the people in contradistinction to the official language of the Church.

25. Cedric Busette, 'Religious Symbolism in Sender's *Mosén Millán*', *Romance Notes*, 11 (1969-70), 482-86. Argues that Paco is a Christ-like figure.

26. M.A. Compitello, '*Réquiem por un campesino español* and the
    Problematics of Exile', in *Homenaje a Ramón J. Sender*, ed. Mary S.
    Vásquez (Newark, Delaware: Juan de la Cuesta, 1987), pp. 87-100.
    Argues that the experience of exile forced Sender into the role of
    'remembrancer' of the Civil War. Suggests that the ballad functions
    in the novel as a textual echo of the literary attempts of exiled writers
    to counter triumphalist versions of the past through 'remembrancing'.

27. Ramón Díaz, 'Mosén Millán de Sender y el padre Rentería de Rulfo:
    semejanza y contraste', in *Studies in Language and Literature: The
    Proceedings of the 23rd Mountain Interstate Foreign Language
    Conference*, ed. Charles L. Nelson (Richmond, Kentucky:
    Department of Foreign Languages, Eastern Kentucky University,
    1976), pp. 143-46. Compares and contrasts the depiction of priests in
    these two novels.

28. Eduardo Godoy Gallardo, 'Problemática y sentido de *Réquiem por un
    campesino español*', *Letras de Deusto*, 1 (1971), 63-74. Analyses
    time and the concept of man's dignity in the novel.

29. Stephen M. Hart, 'Ideology and Narrative Form in Ramón Sender's
    Réquiem por un campesino español and Miguel Delibes's *El
    disputado voto del señor Cayo*', *Quinquereme*, 10 (1987), 207-16.
    Suggests that the ideology of *Réquiem* is articulated neatly through
    the problematical form of the novel.

30. Robert G. Havard, 'The *Romance* in Sender's *Réquiem por un
    campesino español*', *Modern Language Review*, 79 (1984), 88-96.
    Argues that the ballad constitutes a link between the priest's
    memories and the present.

31. David Henn, 'The Priest in Sender's *Réquiem por un campesino
    español*', *International Fiction Review*, 1 (1974), 106-11. Argues that
    Mosén Millán's Christianity is ritualistic rather than ethical.

32. Angel Iglesias Ovejero, 'Estructuras mítico-narrativas de *Réquiem
    por un campesino español*', *Anales de Literatura Española
    Contemporánea*, 7 (1982), 215-36. Discussion of Judas and Christ
    analogies, temporal levels and connotation of proper names in the
    novel.

33. Emiliano Luna Martín, 'La memoria de Mosén Millán: análisis del
    tiempo histórico en el *Réquiem* de Ramón J. Sender', *Revista de
    Literatura*, 48 (1986), 129-35. Identifies the same chronological
    inconsistencies as Raymond Skyrme *(38)*, but argues that they are

introduced deliberately by Sender to underline the fallibility of
Mosén Millán's memory.

34. José Carlos Mainer, 'La culpa y su expiación: dos imágenes en las
novelas de Ramón Sender', *Papeles de Son Armadans*, no. 54 (1969),
117-32. Reviews the images of guilt and expiation in Sender's main
novels.

35. Patricia McDermott, 'Ramón Sender: "Un gran recuerdo típico" ',
Romance Studies, 3 (1983), 47-59. Compares Sender's war diary
Contraataque with *Réquiem*.

36. José Ortega and Francisco Carenas, 'La violencia en *Mosén Millán*',
in *La figura del sacerdote en la moderna narrativa española*, ed.
Ortega and Carenas (Madrid: Casuz, 1975), pp. 107-18. Analyses
how the apparent calm of the village is destroyed by violence,
aggression and war.

37. A. Percival, 'Sociedad, individuo y verdad en *Réquiem por un
campesino español*', *Ottawa Hispánica*, 4 (1982), 71-84. Discusses
the role of *costumbrismo*, realism, myth and truth in Sender's novel.

38. Raymond Skyrme, 'On the Chronology of Sender's *Réquiem por un
campesino español*', *Romance Notes*, 24 (1983-84), 116-22. Finds
two incongruities in the accepted 1911-31 time span of the novel.

LITERARY CRITICISM BY SENDER

39. Ramón J. Sender, *Unamuno, Valle Inclán, Baroja y Santayana.
Ensayos críticos* (México: Ediciones de Andrea, 1955). An uneven
collection of essays. Hostile towards Unamuno, flattering with regard
to Valle Inclán, and dismissive of Baroja's work; argues rather
arbitrarily that Santyana should be considered a member of the 1898
Generation.

40. ----------, *Valle Inclán y la dificultad de la tragedia* (Madrid: Gredos,
1965). Extends some of the ideas of the 1955 essay on Valle Inclán.
Mixes biographical reminiscences with some critical appraisal.

SUPPLEMENTARY BIBLIOGRAPHY

The following critical studies were published after the first edition of the
present critical guide:

41. Martha G. Krow-Lucal, 'El esperpento de Mosén Millán: A
reflection of Valle-Inclán in Sender', *Hispanic Review*, 61 (1993),

391–402. Compares the use of the 'esperpento' technique in Valle-Inclán's *Los cuernos de don Friolera* with Sender's novel. Argues that there is a similarity in the presentation of a story and its characters from three different points of view, in the contribution of Spanish history to the storyline, and in the depiction of the tyranny of traditional social roles.

42. Juan Fernández Jiménez, 'Autodecepción y desengaño en *Mosén Millán*', *Cuadernos de ALDEEU*, 5 (1989), 241–48. Argues that Mosén Millán made a mistake in betraying Paco and that he was prey to self-deception.

43. Mercedes Junquera, 'La temática de la guerra civil en Ramón J. Sender', *Cuadernos de ALDEEU*, 5 (1989), 249–56. Section on *Réquiem* (pp. 253–56) argues that Sender goes beyond history in his novel in order to address universal ethical problems.

44. Charles L. King, 'Recent Research on Ramón Sender', *España Contemporánea*, 1 (1988), 157–64. Updates previous bibliographic work, and gives a positive review of two articles on *Réquiem* by Havard (*30*) and Iglesias Ovejero (*32*) (p.169).

45. Kevin S. Larsen, 'Betrayal and Bad Faith: Sartre's "Le Mur" and Sender's *Réquiem por un campesino español*', *Crítica Hispánica*, 10 (1988), 93–105. Sees similarity between Mosén Millán and the protagonist of Sartre's short story, Pablo, in their role as father figures and in their 'mauvaise foi'.

46. Patricia McDermott (ed.), 'Ramón J. Sender: *Réquiem por un campesino español*' (Manchester: Manchester University Press, 1991). Contains an excellent introduction (pp.1-40) which is sensitive to the historical and religious resonances of the novel's imagery, as well as the connotations of the protagonists' names.

47. José M. Pérez Carrera, 'Guía de lectura de *Réquiem por un campesino español*' (Madrid: Akal, 1988). A basic introduction to the main themes of the novel, providing hints on how to dramatize scenes from the novel in the classroom. Has a helpful map of the time sequence (p.8), a useful comparison between *Réquiem* and José Ramón Arana's *El cura de Almuniaced* (pp.59–66), and a very good section on the language of Sender's novel, including Aragonisms, colloquialisms and ungrammaticalities (pp.67–73).

48. María del Carmen Porrúa, 'Tres novelas de la guerra civil', *Cuadernos Hispanoamericanos*, 473–74 (1989), 45–57. Section on *Réquiem* (pp.52–54) emphasizes the symbolic, representative nature of the conflict and the characters.

CRITICAL GUIDES TO SPANISH TEXTS

Edited by
J.E. Varey, A.D. Deyermond & C. Davies

CRITICAL GUIDES TO SPANISH TEXTS

Edited by
J.E. Varey, A.D. Deyermond & C. Davies